MOTHERS of PRIESTS

Rev. Fr. Robert Quardt, SCJ

ANGELUS PRESS
2915 Forest Avenue, Kansas City, MO 64109

Original title: *Priestermütter*
Translated from the German for Angelus Press by
Marc S. Fisher; edited by Angelus Press.

Crucifixion cover artwork: Nathan Rush, Leonardo's Art Studio
Poetry: *The Priest's Mother* by Elisabeth Mayer

NIHIL OBSTAT: Stegen, June 7, 1956. P. Leo Kunz, SCJ,
   librorum cens.
IMPRIMI POTEST: Oberkassel, June 15, 1956. P. H. Krolage,
   Sup. prov.

NIHIL OBSTAT: Fr. M.-St. Morard, O.P., librorum cens.
IMPRIMATUR: Friburgi Helv., December 1, 1959. L. Waever,
   vic. gen.

ANGELUS PRESS
2915 FOREST AVENUE
KANSAS CITY, MISSOURI 64109
PHONE (816) 753-3150
FAX (816) 753-3557
ORDER LINE 1-800-966-7337

ISBN 0-935952-56-X
FIRST PRINTING—April 1995
SECOND PRINTING—February 2003

Printed in the United States of America

Contents

Introduction

From Pope Pius X comes the statement: "*A vocation comes from the heart of God, but goes through the heart of the mother.*" That these words correspond to the facts is demonstrated by experience. One need only inquire once of the priests from the rank and file, and the majority of them will corroborate the statement of the saintly pope, namely, that next to God, they have their good mother or grandmother to thank for their priestly vocation. In the chapters that follow are a few examples, which history has handed down, to confirm the statement of Pope St. Pius X.

I did not know that peace could pass
When life had gained a sudden goal—
So old, the solaced thought that he
To God would give his silent soul....

Saint Monica

As the first in this series of mothers of priests, this story produces the irrefutable proof that the influence of the mother on the development of the priestly vocation is extremely important. That a decadent and immoral young man became a holy priest and bishop, Augustine, whose work endures even today was, next to the grace of God, the work of his mother.

If Monica was such a good mother, how was it that Augustine went astray?

The first reason lies in his divided upbringing. In the 4th century, the time in which Monica lived, the Christians were still very thinly spread and mixed marriages were very common. Very seldom, however, was a mixed marriage to become as regrettable and deplorable as the one which the eighteen-year-old Monica entered into with the municipal employee, Patricius, who was twice her age. He was a heathen, a purely secular man, unrestrained in his excesses and, what is more, irritable, violent, and boisterous.

So long as the mother oversaw his upbringing, Augustine was a well-behaved child. The circumstances changed, however, as the father interfered. For him, piety and a fine mind were not the goals of the education of his well-endowed eldest son, but rather worldly fame and fortune. He consciously and systematically snatched from the children the Christian purity and modesty which Monica had so diligently and carefully planted. The nasty husband did not even have qualms about putting the religious ideas of the mother up to ridicule before the son. But whenever in a family like this the father shouts "giddy up" and the mother "whoa," the child doesn't know at first whom he should follow until the stronger side wins and, with growing sons, the father will be the winner most of the time. So, Augustine let fall the guiding hand of his mother and followed his father from the mountain into the abyss.

A second cause as to why Augustine became an immoral man lies in the nature and character of young men. Monica's son was quite intelligent, the teacher's pet, who outshone all of his fellow students with his knowledge. Early on he was considered a popular poet and an admirable speaker. Plenty of attention was given him from many sides and, as is commonly the case, this went right to his head. An excessive pride took possession of him resulting, as it often does, in a rampage of sensuous desires overcoming his weakened will to resist. In Augustine, as so often is the case with impressionable young men, immorality followed pride. School and acquaintances brought to completion what began in pride and his divided upbringing. Of his deplorable school days, the converted Augustine was to write later these significant words: "From the golden chalice I drank poison, which was brought to me by enchanted teachers." Books, theater, and bad company did the rest. And, when a child was born to Augustine out of wedlock, it was not the name of the father, Augustine, which suffered, but of his mother. The entire city spoke of Monica's son, and to her came disgrace and dishonor. Despite this, Augustine still praised himself, out of megalomania, in the circle of his like-minded immoral friends, in order to be considered the worst among them.

Augustine himself would later often remark on the errors of these ways of his youth. But how could it happen that this rotten youth could develop into a holy priest and bishop?

Again, it is he himself who answers this question with these words so full of meaning: "For what I became and what I am, I thank my mother for her prayers and merits."

But how did Monica, for her part, help turn her son around?

Monica's husband—to complete the story—converted under the influence of his holy wife one year before his death and became a complete and devoted Christian. Over its last twelve months, this dark, dismal marriage was filled with bright sunshine.

In order to foster the same conversion in her son, Monica tried, as do mothers even today in the same situation, to bring her son back through good exhortations. Obviously she met with no success, for young people who fall to the dogs are in no way open to pious sayings. They perceive such words as annoyances, for as the converted Augustine remarked later, "I had cast these motherly admonitions into the wind as the silly babble of a woman."

The persistent Monica made other attempts to convince her son by entering into learned disputes with him. But, the modest and simple woman always came up short because learnedness was one-sidedly with her son. It was easy for

Augustine to refute the assertions of his mother through hairsplitting arguments and often he sharply ridiculed the dear woman. These disputes were fruitless, too. The day finally came when Monica did the exact opposite of attending so acutely to her son. Surely she must have dreaded the thought of it. She threw Augustine out of the house. She told him that she could no longer live under the same roof and eat at the same table with him. Always the mother, she gave him her savings before sending him off. But despite this motherly generosity, returning harshness with harshness seldom does good, because it often only enlarges the heap of shambles. Monica soon saw this, and called her son back home.

In the time following, Monica tried to accomplish what she was not able to achieve by enlisting the help of another person. She thought that where she wasn't able to convert her son, a bishop she had befriended might be successful. But, alas, this was again a way which rarely leads to the conversion of souls like Augustine's. Such young people given to sin and inflated by pride hardly ever are stirred to reformation through persuasion. They perceive the aim and become annoyed. For every good word they have, they have three bad ones ready; and before someone can even get near them, they are long gone. For this reason, the bishop rejected Monica's request as unfeasible and bound to fail. He gave only one consolation to the weeping mother as he said to her, "Mother Monica, let him go, and be satisfied to pray for him. As surely as you are living, it is not possible that the son of these tears should perish."

Thus spoke the bishop, and he was proved to be right in the end.

So far, none of Monica's four ways had won her son's conversion. Only one last resort remained: that way which the bishop had shown to her, the way of prayer by which, with the help of God, the spiritually dead son would be awakened to new life. Monica now entered upon this way, and on she went, untiringly, for eighteen years. Against all hope and in spite of many setbacks, the woman prayed on persistently and without ceasing until God's hour of grace finally struck. Who could have known that the faithful and trusting prayer of this mother would be answered in a more glorious way than she could have ever imagined, for Augustine would convert so profoundly and completely that he would become a Saint, who as a priest and bishop would be counted for all time as one of the very greatest in the Catholic Church.

With Augustine's conversion, Monica's longsuffering prayers were answered. The joy, however, which came over her was so vehement that the old heart of the mother couldn't take it. A short time later she died. Ever since, Monica's life has constituted the irrefutable evidence that mothers, moved to God's will, can obtain by prayer a holy priest from a decadent son. Mothers, indeed, have a great influence on the development of a priestly vocation.

"What I became and what I am," says the holy Augustine, "I owe to the prayers and merits of my mother."

...Yet with the low-declared desire
To answer to the awesome sign,
I could have prayed to Mary's Son
To let his days be dwelt with mine!

Alice of Montbard

One knows neither the year nor the day when Alice of Montbard, a descendant of a French noble family, was born. Of her early death at the age of around thirty-five, one only knows that it fell in the year 1106 or 1107. Alice's parents had promised the child to God before birth according to medieval custom. The little daughter fully understood the solemn parental vow as she grew up, but she came upon love, however, in the form of the young baron named Fegelin de Fontaine-les-Dijon. The heart of the young maiden caught fire, and Alice soon came to the belief that she was destined for marriage. However, because she also wanted to respect the solemn vow of her parents, she proposed to God that she would consecrate all of the children He would give her as a substitute in her place. One is tempted to smile at this young girl. We can imagine that God, however, did not smile, but we will see He was to pay Himself handsomely on the offer! In turn, the couple brought seven children into the world within a few years. First, there were three boys: Guido, Gerhard, and Bernard. Exactly in the middle came a girl, Humbelina. Finally, there were three more boys: Andrew, Bartholomew, and Nivard. In the nursery of the palace of Fontaine-les-Dijon, however, most of the time it was louder than loud, as five of the boys took after their warlike father. War games, gymnastics, fencing, and riding filled the day to the brim. Only Bernard, the third eldest, was a quiet child, bashful and shy. He was clumsy in daily life, and much too serious for his age. Still he got along best with his mother, and when she died while he was away at school, Bernard was no more attracted to the world.

The twenty-two-year-old was drawn strongly to the cloister, and, as his plan met the opposition of his father and brothers, he showed that he, too, the shy young man, was of knightly stock. He was a Christian knight, and a Knight of Mary, noble, well-bred, and proud who, with his bright enthusiasm, set his family and neighborhood on fire, so that he did not leave the world alone, but on the contrary, he took one uncle and four brothers, and even twenty noble landowners from the castles all around, and moved them to exchange the knight's armor for the monk's cowl.

As the five brothers took leave of the castle that was their home, Guido, the eldest, said to Nivard, the youngest, who was still a child and who stayed behind: "Look, all of our belongings are now for you alone."

Then Nivard replied: "I do not accept the exchange, for you leave me fleeting goods and chattels, and you seek heaven for yourselves."

A few weeks later, Nivard, too, followed the brothers. The sister likewise entered the convent. Finally the elderly father, Fegelin de Fontaine-les-Dijon, joined the sons, and would soon himself become a monk!

God made into a spectacular good the offer Alice of Montbard made to Him. The names of her sons, Bernard, Gerhard, and Nivard (as well as that of her husband, Fegelin), stand today in the ranks of the saints of the Church. Alice's greatest glory, however, is Bernard, one of the greatest saints of the Catholic Church.

His soul is prone before the throne
In blind oblation to the Cross;
What grace in ardor's recompense!
What wonder won in worldly loss!..

Alice Rolls

So much like the Frenchwoman Alice de Montbard and yet so different, is the life of the Englishwoman Alice Rolls, who gave birth to thirteen children of whom ten consecrated themselves to the religious life. This fact is remarkable, for Alice Rolls came from a Protestant family and was raised in Protestantism. Even more astounding is our knowledge that Alice Rolls converted selfishly to the Catholic Faith simply because she desired to marry a Catholic. Now we know that the consequences of such conversions from purely exterior motives are usually not beneficial. As is well-known, love blinds, and soon the illusion of love fades away. On the other hand, one can still be happy on the point that at least the Catholic upbringing of the children is guaranteed.

But with Alice Rolls, the usual drawbacks of such a conversion did not develop. Her conversion to Mother Church, which occurred just days before her wedding (1830), was not to be just another name on paper, but was a profound interior conversion which truly overcame all the disdain and evil animosities of her old Protestant self. She became by all accounts a full-blooded Catholic woman.

This complete change of heart was aided in no small way by the fact that Alice Rolls married into the Vaughn family—Catholic through and through, ancestors of which refused to become Protestant at the time of the English Catholic persecution under Queen Elizabeth I and accepted dungeons and expropriations rather than betray the Catholic Faith. Throughout the decades of those dangerous but also extremely glorious days Courtfield was the ancestral castle of the Vaughns. It was the place of refuge and the hiding place of the hunted priests who, in every possible disguise, in spite of constant threat of martyrdom, operated throughout the land. Especially because of the great number of Holy Masses celebrated secretly there, Courtfield was considered a kind of holy place. Indeed, while this glorious and heroic time was almost three hundred years past, the Catholic sense of the Vaughn family had not changed. Three sons and three daughters chose the religious life as their vocation, while the heir of the castle, Colonel Vaughn, was to become the husband of Alice Rolls.

As was already mentioned, the young lady became Catholic with her whole heart, and the religious zeal, as one often encounters with genuine converts, urged her on with her like-minded spouse to make the proposal to raise all of the children they would be given for the possibility of God's service.

Colonel Vaughn gladly assented to the desire of his wife, and God gave the holy wish of the married couple superabundant fulfillment. Ten of the thirteen children received the grace of priestly or religious vocations. As with St. Bernard and his siblings, so it was in the Vaughn family that the priestly heart of the mother was the source of all those grace-filled vocations.

Alice Rolls knew how to make the religious education of the children extremely attractive. She loved to tell the venerable legends of the heroes and heroines of the Faith and to her children thereby the saints became like trusted friends and family. It is said that as one of the children held a clock to his ear and listened to it, the mother said, "Look, life passes like this tick-tock. When, however, our heart stops with the strike of death, almighty God winds it up again, for He wills that we live with him forever."

On the frequent charitable journeys to the needy in the neighborhood, the mother gladly allowed herself to be accompanied by one or another of her children and she instructed them for their part to give some of their savings or toys to the poor.

With Herbert, the eldest, the priestly vocation made itself known when he was sixteen years old. As he broke the news to his mother she replied smiling, "Child, I've known that for a long time."

Colonel Vaughn was apparently less pleased about the news, as he had hoped all along that the eldest would someday become a high-ranking officer in the English army. Nevertheless, he also bowed to the will of God Who took from him the son that would years later become a prince of the Church. Almost prophetic regarding the influence of Herbert's decision, he wrote in a letter to a friend at the time the words: "When Herbert goes, all the others will go as well."

So he wrote. Not all went, but almost all.

At the age of nineteen Herbert moved to Rome, the center of Christendom, there to draw from the clearest fountains of Catholic scholarship. Two years later, while he was still away, his mother died shortly after having delivered her thirteenth child. Death surprised her suddenly at evening prayers. Of the children who had come from her fruitful womb and been nurtured by her generous heart, she would see no more on this earth.

What became then of her children?

Francis and Reginald married, continued the family line, and gave the world examples of genuine Christian family life.

Margaret remained single, stayed in her family's house, and finally moved to a convent, where she died.

Of the remaining four daughters, Gladys entered the Visitation Nuns, Thérèse became a Sister of Mercy, Clara, a Poor Clare, and Maria, an Augustinian.

The rest of her six sons were ordained priests.

Kenelm became a secular priest and was later the right hand and strongest supporter of his great eldest brother, Herbert.

Joseph entered the Benedictines and laid the ground for a new abbey.

Bernard became a Jesuit and a speaker of some renown. As he danced at a ball on the day before he entered the Society, he said to his familiar dance partner that she would be his last as he was going to become a Jesuit. Astonished and shocked at the same time, the bewildered woman remarked, "But please! You want to become a Jesuit? You, who love the world and dance so well?" The noble reply ran something like this: "Even for that very reason, I consecrate myself to God."

Next followed Roger, who with Joseph became a Benedictine. He was later entrusted with the offices of Novicemaster and then Prior. When he was forty, the pope elevated him to Archbishop of Sydney, where he built a magnificent cathedral.

John, the youngest, became bishop of Salford in England. He was a learned man who wrote twenty books.

Alice Rolls earned the greatest honor, however, with Herbert, the eldest. At the age of twenty-two he received the holy priesthood in Rome. After his return to his homeland, he entered the Oratory of St. Philip Neri. Soon after, he was named by the bishop to be the acting rector of the London seminary. A few years later, the venturesome priest founded, against incredible difficulties, two missionary societies, one for men and one for women, at Mill Hill near London. Today they work very fruitfully in five continents for the conversion of the heathen.

At forty, Herbert Vaughn was raised to the Bishopric of Salford, which he later exchanged for the episcopal see of Manchester and, after the death of Cardinal Manning, he became the Archbishop of Westminster in 1892. Not quite a year later, he was named to the College of Cardinals by Pope Leo XIII.

In examining what the Catholic Church of today in England is and signifies, one may look in large part to the work of Herbert, the eldest son of Alice Rolls, the Protestant who became a Catholic with her whole heart, and from this priestly heart gave ten of thirteen children to God: five nuns, two religious priests, one bishop, one archbishop, and one cardinal.

From the Frenchman René Bazin come the words, "There are mothers with priestly souls which they transmit to their children."

Shame on us that the current shortage of priests, at least in part, might follow from the fact that there are so few priestly mothers like Alice Rolls.

... Tensely he kneels to take the seals;
Above his brow the chalice glows;
The babe that rested on my breast
Upon his way Anointed goes!

Margherita Ochiena

An event from her childhood shows in a flash from which
wood Margherita Ochiena was cut. War reigned in the land,
and as the nine-year-old was home alone one day, enemy
soldiers came to her parents' farm and drove their horses to
the open floor of the barn where they put them to eating the
family's good harvested oats. Margherita begged the intrud-
ers to be considerate of the meager harvest. The soldiers,
however, laughed and acted as if they didn't understand her
dialect. In response, the fearless girl took a pitchfork and
chased the horses out of the barn! Of such form was
Margherita Ochiena even as a child, and so she stayed her
entire life: determined, courageous, and energetic.

In 1812, at the age of twenty-four, Margherita married a
widower who brought with him a nine-year-old son and his
sickly, elderly mother. She herself gave birth to two more
sons. Just five years after their wedding, her husband died
after four days of illness. The young widow worked doubly

hard to maintain the family's small farming operation. She plowed, planted, reaped and banded the bundles, loaded them onto the wagon, brought them home, thrashed the grain, and brought the corn to the silo—all by herself! The excessive work and cares in no way hindered Margherita in her care of the elderly mother-in-law, whom she unreservedly submitted to, or her stepson and her own two children, all of whom she loved equally. The stepson, who later became an exemplary individual, gave her a lot of grief. He was surly, envious, and complained unfairly that Margherita put her own children before him. Without her husband, it became difficult to keep the boys happy.

As Margherita's training was inspired by a warm kindheartedness tempered with firmness and quiet strength, so she always prevailed when the children were guilty of wrongdoing. On a wall in the living room hung as a constant warning the rod which, though seldom used, sometimes became active.

Margherita's upbringing of the children was completely and entirely focused on religion. Above all she taught them to be aware of the omnipresence of God. She would show the children that God sees everything, both what is thought and what is done. She permitted the children to play with other children but she took care to say, "Yes, just play, but remember that God sees you!" She read in the face of one of the boys that he was angry so she whispered in his ear, "God sees even your most secret thoughts." Experience taught her that to pardon a naughty child whom she knew had been lying, she should confront him face to face. Before the liar could say a word she would say, "Do not speak except thereby to think that God sees you." In this way, Margherita impressed deeply on the boys the awareness of the presence of God. It would be wise to heed a mother who raises her children to have such a well-formed conscience.

Once she had been wronged by a wayward neighborhood boy in a major way and in public. Pitying the condition of his soul, Margherita said to her boys, "If I knew that you would turn out like that, I would ask God to let you die on the spot!" From the mouth of a mother such words sound harsh, but just for that reason they guide so much more effectively the inclinations of the children away from the evil and towards the good.

One day Margherita's heartfelt wish, which she had so long cherished in silence, seemed to be fulfilled. Hans, the youngest, confided to her that he would like to become a priest. In that instant the mother's heart fluttered for joy, but from the lips of the prudent woman came the dry words, "Priest...priest...that is quickly said. Why do you want to become a priest?"

With this almost too-sharp reply the short talk abruptly ended and the nine-year-old Hans had in the meantime to think about the reasons he wanted to become a priest. Margherita was far removed from favoring the youngest because of his plans, for it was clear to her from the beginning that the vocation must prove itself, and the trials to test it did not wait long.

Scarcely had the now twenty-year-old stepbrother gotten wind of the matter that he immediately moved with all his strength against the plan. Like a little spoiled child, he teased Hans about it every day. "Only the Lord allows such laziness! Would Hans be happy as such a lord, too? Priests are lazy!" Thereafter, the eldest no longer called the youngest by name, but insulted him whenever he found any opportunity to do so, with the mocking calls "Little Lord" or "Lord Doctor." So persistent and wild was the stepbrother that Margherita advised Hans to seek food, shelter, and money elsewhere.

Hans became a cow herdsman and farm hand. He also possessed skills in other useful areas. He learned tailoring and cabinetmaking, and did still other jobs in order to get through life. At the same time he also studied. Because he was a splendid student, he finished his preparatory studies, in spite of all obstacles, at twenty years of age. When he took leave of his mother before his entrance into the seminary, already in clerical dress, Margherita said to him in her straightforward way, "True, I am happy that you have succeeded thus far, but remember that the clothes don't make the priest, and should serious doubts come to you about your vocation before ordination, then you must necessarily take off the garb and lay it aside. I would much rather you remain your entire life a farmhand than that you become an unworthy priest. You do not need to worry about my future. I was born poor, I have lived poor, and I shall also die poor. I desire nothing from you, and if you should strive to become a wealthy pastor, believe me, I shall not step foot over the threshold of your house. Mark my words!"

As Margherita's son received the holy priesthood six years later, his mother said to him after his first Mass: "You will now pray for me every morning at the Holy Sacrifice. Otherwise, I ask nothing of you. In no way do you need to worry about me. Care first for the souls entrusted to you."

Of such uprightness and pure intentions was this mother, Margherita. Did the son of this priestly woman become a priest of some importance? That he became such his name alone proves. His name is John Bosco.

The young priest directed himself according to the example set by his noble mother. Incredibly poor working conditions prevailed in the great working-class city of Turin, Italy. There were children there in gangs who, begging and idle in

tattered clothing, moved through the city, spending the night
under gateways and bridges and stealing like the magpies.
Depraved and corrupted, they lived among dirty talk, in a
troubled land, with troubled people. Don Bosco went among
them, accepting them in every respect. He founded a home
for them and gave them nourishment, clothing, a place to
live, and education. As he was over his head in work in a
short time, he stood before his mother one day at home,
described his situation to her, and asked her to move in with
him and take over the household with the neglected boys.
Silently Margherita listened to the account of her son, considered it for a short time, then a bright light shone from her
good eyes, and the sixty-year-old said, "If you believe that
your work is God's will, then you can count on me."

The next day, the two walked the long road to Turin. A
little laundry was all the mother brought from home. Determined, spirited, and energetic, Margherita took up her difficult service. She had laboriously raised three children, and
now, as an old woman, she must be a mother to hundreds in
the course of the next years. This she did untiringly. Day
after day, year after year, she cooked, washed, and sewed for
the foster children of her son, although for her the sacrifices
which she made from unselfish motherliness for a depraved
society would very often be paid back with malicious thank-
lessness. The heroic woman lost her nerve only once. She
was in fact and quite really on the edge of her strength as she
then said to her son, "I'm finished. This is the end. Yesterday
the boys ripped the wash from the line and dragged it through
the mud again. They trampled the fresh vegetables in the
garden. They so damage their clothes with their mischief
that I no longer know how I should repair them. They lose
their shoes and socks. Every second they hide dishes in the
kitchen, so that I have to search hours for them. I quit, I

quit, I quit! I am going home so that I might still find a little peace in my old age."

Thus spoke Mother Margherita in a time of great irritation, the first time in her long and difficult life that she complained so bitterly. The son let his mother speak out without interruption, and listened silently and, as she finished, he beckoned quietly to the cross on the bare wall. Margherita understood the gesture instantly. With a resigned look on her venerable old face and tears in her eyes, she said in a sorrowful voice, "Child, you are right. I had not thought of that." So she spoke, and turned quietly back to her harsh and thankless work, and stayed at her post until she drew her last breath.

Mother and son were indispensable to each other.

Over time, Don Bosco's work slowly expanded. The home in Turin developed into a veritable city. There were always a thousand pupils lodged there. Elsewhere, new institutions of his foundations were made in Italy, France, England, Belgium, Holland, Spain, Portugal, Germany, Austria, Switzerland, Turkey, Poland, Hungary, America, Asia, Africa, and Australia—all over the world.

Indeed, sugary consolations were not for Mother Margherita. She suffered through the many difficult years of her son's apostolate, side by side with him, without glory nor fanfare. In the year 1856, now seventy years old, Margherita contracted pneumonia. The overworked and undernourished body of the old woman could no longer mount resistance to illness. The end of this glorious life was drawing to a close.

"Child," the dying woman said, "before I helped you to receive the sacraments. Now it is up to you to help me. Bring me the Holy Viaticum and administer Extreme Unction. I soon will no longer be able to pray aloud. So, pray the prayers

slowly and clearly, that I might pray with you in my heart."
Mother Margherita was herself even in the hour of death.
What she was in life—resolute, spirited, and energetic—so
she was in death.

Her last night alive came. The son watched sorrowfully
by the deathbed. His mother looked him straight in the eyes
and said, "You suffer. For that reason, leave me! Go and pray!
Whatever we have left to discuss, will be understood in eternity."

Crying, Don Bosco retorted, "No, mother, let me stay
with you! In this hour, I cannot leave you!"

In a hushed tone, Margherita replied from her deathbed: "You go. I beg you, do me this favor. It is my last wish.
My suffering is doubled when I see you suffering. So, go! I
have help enough. Go and pray for me! I really want nothing. Till we meet again!..."

Thus spoke Margherita, and so Don Bosco obeyed her
this last time and left her in peace. One can understand how
Don Bosco, when he was shortly thereafter informed of the
death of his mother, broke uncontrollably into tears.

The reason St. John Bosco became a model priest, whose
blessed work spans the world and transcends time, is not
hard to find. He had a model mother whose priestly heart
she had communicated to her son.

One can understand why those who knew Don Bosco's
mother called her, "Margherita the Great."

To God's still steps he bears the Book;
His worn face whitens as he slips
The ribboned leaves. He lifts his hand!
The Word comes firmly from his lips!..

Frau Neuenhofen

The chaplain of a prison stumbled into the cell of a convict. The prisoner drew the attention of the priest to the graffiti sign which he himself had scrawled and which hung on the whitewashed wall. The sign read: "Mothers are the Fate of Men."

"You see, Father," said the convict, "in prison one has time to think about a lot of things, and the result of my reflection is this small saying: 'Mothers are the Fate of Men.' A good mother is a blessing for the children; a bad mother, however, is a terrible curse."

The man said no more, and the priest tactfully did not inquire further.

Why is this event related here even though it may sound out of place? For the very reason that in the mirror of contrast, truth becomes much more bright and certain.

Mothers are the fate of men and, we must say, the fate of priests.

Vorst is a great market town in the vicinity of the Rhine city of Krefeld, West Germany. A hundred and forty years ago, an eighteen-year-old girl was taken sick there in a very bad way. Already near to death, the dying girl made the vow that if she was given the grace to overcome the illness and later to be married, she would consecrate her firstborn child to the exclusive service of God.

The *fraulein* recovered and seven years later she married. During those seven years, Frau Neuenhofen, as she was called after her marriage, never forgot her promise. At the moment she knew that God had blessed her with a child, she offered it as Mary herself would have done while the divine Child slept in the holy cradle beneath her heart. Frau Neuenhofen renewed her offering every day. Her first child was to be a boy, and some say in retrospect that it appeared the child was already given a miraculous pre-disposition to the priesthood while in the sanctuary of his mother's womb. Already early on his priestly vocation was known to him, and his mother prudently guarded him carefully from every harmful influence. In Steyl (1885), he received the holy priesthood.

On the evening of the day of his First Mass, the happy mother walked with her son through the garden. On this occasion, Frau Neuenhofen spoke for the first time of her promise, which she had carried silently in her heart all these years, and she ended the conversation with these words: "God is good. You are now a priest. This morning I received from your hand the Body of Christ. Soon, your brother John will be ordained as well, and, if all is as it seems, our youngest will eventually become a priest."

Thus spoke so confidently the priestly woman, and it later came to pass. I say "priestly woman," because she had the zeal for souls which characterizes priests. Three sons of

Frau Neuenhofen became priests. The eldest was a spiritual director and teacher to priests and future priests. Among his many students were three missionary bishops. What blessings came forth from this mother with the priestly heart for the salvation of souls, and, by extension, from the sons she gave to the holy priesthood of her Lord Jesus Christ!

"Mothers are the fate of men."

We have to admit this statement does not always hold true. There is another saying, "Like father, like son," and indeed now and then one or another boy will follow his father over the cliff into the deep water. The writer of these lines remembers his visit to a prison camp during World War II. A convict who had spent sixteen of his forty-eight years behind bars once said to me in a remorseful tone: "You know, Fr. Robert, I come from a good family. My mother goes to Mass every day. All of my brothers and sisters are upright and highly regarded. I alone am the black sheep at home, the greatest sorrow of my old mother."

Not always are mothers the fate of men, but the decision about the priesthood of one or more of her sons most always lies with the mother.

How did the holy Pope Pius X put it?..."A vocation to the priestly state," he maintained, "comes from the heart of God, but comes through the heart of the mother."

...Oh, Michael, send thy mighty sword!
Oh, gracious Gabriel, convey
Thy spirit to his speech! Oh, Love,
Let fall thy rain of flame today!

Margherita Sanson

Entering into marriage on February 13, 1833, the seam-stress Margherita Sanson signed the marriage certificate with a small cross, as was the custom of the time, for she could neither read nor write. Her new husband was a civil servant with a daily wage of one single franc (about twenty cents US in 1995 exchange rates). Besides that, he had so little land that he could cultivate it with his only cow from which, moreover, was required the daily milk.

That was the entire estate, and on this estate in the course of the next twenty years ten children were born, of which, in spite of the thin slices of bread and the pitifully ragged cloth-ing, eight survived. This feat was achieved only for the very reason that, as the father lived extremely frugally and mod-estly, the mother, often until late in the night, sewed for other people. Of the father we know he attended Holy Mass daily and read the lives of the saints to the children every night.

On the day of his first Holy Communion, Joseph, the eldest son of the family, decided God had called him to the priesthood. Although he intended to keep his decision a secret, Margherita quickly discovered the secret, and from that same hour on the little boy found the strongest support for the realization of his calling from his mother. The father, however, even with all his piety, was not as enthusiastic for this plan. He already figured that the oldest son would soon help with the support of the large family. After all, where would the money come from for his studies? So thought rightly the reasonable father, but the faithful mother prevailed over his thoughts by trusting the matter to God's providence.

Steadfastly trusting in this Providence, Joseph began his studies. First thing each day, his local priest drilled him in the rudiments of the Latin language. Then Margherita's son walked almost an hour to the higher school in the next town. He literally "took the road under his feet" because, in order to save the soles, he would dangle his shoes by their laces over his shoulder. Only when he was nearly at school did he actually put his shoes on. In springtime, Joseph would rest a while by the spring along the school-route. Fresh watercress grew here and he would lay the watercress as filling between the slices of bread he would save from morning breakfast.

He admirably tested and proved God's providence throughout the year. When the preparatory studies were finally over, it was again this Providence, without which this young man could never realize the priesthood, which provided a scholarship to the seminary.

And so the goal was brought nearer to hand. But then Margherita's husband died suddenly leaving behind for the forty-year-old widow nine destitute children, of whom the youngest at only four days of age was to soon exchange its life on earth for that of heaven.

It was immediately clear to Joseph that under these circumstances he could not cost his mother a penny more. For that reason, he said to her after the burial of his father: "Mother, now I lay my studies aside and help you with the upbringing and care of my brothers and sisters." "You stupid boy," she shouted in answer, "have you forgotten that God has called you? You will continue your studies, and that is that!"

Margherita's son returned to the seminary and his enterprising mother called together the two eldest daughters, aged thirteen and eleven, to join her in sewing more diligently for the neighbors.

Six years later, on September 18, 1858, the son of a seamstress was ordained to the holy priesthood and celebrated his first Solemn Mass the following day in his hometown. In her son of twenty-three years, the will of God for which she had prayed, worked, and sacrificed was accomplished.

Margherita's son became a curate with an income which scarcely sufficed to meet his own needs. As he very quickly acquired a reputation as an outstanding preacher, he was frequently invited to give feast day sermons in neighboring parishes. He gave the honorariums, which were often slipped into his hands on such occasions, to his mother, unless he came upon someone poorer beforehand who needed the support more than his own family. Then, he excused himself well with the words, "You know, mother, Providence needed the money in this case for the poor, in comparison to whom you are truly rich."

Margherita's response was usually a kindhearted and knowing smile, "Beppi, I am so happy that you are a just priest."

After nine years as an assistant, Margherita's son became

a pastor. The paltry furniture which he brought with him and which barely filled a single room of the rectory aroused an uncharitable judgment from the parishioners regarding the new pastor. One even remarked: "Hey, what's the bishop trying to do to us by sending us one like *him*?!"

This rash judgment would quickly be destroyed. Soon the unanimous conviction of all six thousand souls in the parish was that no one could have a better pastor. It was especially the magnanimous charity and genuine priestly care of the sick by which the priest conquered hearts.

Nine years later, the bishop named Margherita's son a cathedral canon, chancellor of the diocese, and spiritual director of the seminary. After another nine years, this son of a civil servant and seamstress was himself made bishop.

Shortly after his episcopal consecration, dressed entirely in purple, with a golden cross on his chest and a ring encrusted with precious stones on his finger, the new fifty-year-old prince of the Church visited his then seventy-year-old mother—his mother who in the meantime, without the help he had offered, raised seven children to be fine men and women. Mother and son affectionately greeted each other. Both overcome with joyful tears by this memorable reunion, the new bishop said jokingly to his mother, "Look at the handsome ring someone gave me!" Margherita then, as she was bidden to do, reverently kissed the symbol of episcopal dignity. She then, becoming reflective, and pointing to her simple silver wedding band, the old woman said with emphasis: "Surely, Beppi, your ring is beautiful, but you would not be wearing it today, had I not first worn this wedding ring."

The bishop then bowed his head over Margherita's hand, reverently kissed the symbol of her marital and motherly dignity, and as he rose up, a childlike tear of thanks shone as a pearl of great price on her wedding ring.

The busy and responsible position which Margherita's son held as bishop changed nothing in the trusting relationship with his mother, but it meant that he seldom turned up at home for a visit, as was previously the case, and when he did visit, he would no sooner arrive than he had to leave. It is understandable that mother Margherita was a little annoyed by that, and in a feigned ill temper she took the opportunity to say, "Yes, yes, Beppi, there's not much good for you, I guess, in a little old woman as I am now."

Then one day the bishop arrived at home unexpectedly and unannounced, and to the question of how long he would stay this time, he answered, "I am staying here the entire month."

With these words, the heart of the seventy-five-year-old woman fluttered for a second, and great joy showed over her wrinkled face. She remained so for the long four weeks during which she had her Beppi with her, and took him as before under her secure wings.

Margherita looked after her son as in the days of his boyhood, and when she kidded how Beppi, who, from childhood on, was a little thick between the ears, he laughed heartily, so comfortable and unaffected was the relationship between the mother and her episcopal son.

Nine years after his episcopal consecration, Beppi scheduled a trip into the country on the occasion of receiving the cardinalate (1893) to visit his now eighty-year-old mother for the last time. He was now dressed completely in red. The child of a seamstress had been made a cardinal of the Holy Roman Church. In the humble apartment, the two sat facing each other. Sunshine streamed through the window. Its light was caught in the crackling purple silk of the cardinal's robe. A brightness like fire flashed through the small room, and from the grey whitewashed walls came a light reflection onto the paltry furniture. As if blinded by all the pomp, Margherita shaded her old, weak eyes with her hand. Then the eighty-year-old drew nearer to her son, the sixty-year-old, and the old seamstress said to the cardinal of the Holy Roman Church: "Child, for me, be not too proud!"

Soon thereafter, in 1894, mother Margherita died. Had she lived nine years longer, she would have seen her son dressed in white with a three-tiered crown upon his head. Her Beppi was now pope! It may be safe to presume that the simple woman saw this day in the hereafter. As well, united with her children in eternal happiness, she celebrated yet another glorious day, namely, May 29, 1954, when Pope Pius XII canonized her eldest son, Pope St. Pius X.

Margherita Sarto, née Sanson, the mother of the holy Pope Pius X, is an outstanding model for all mothers whose heartfelt desire is to want the will of God for their children, even if it be that His will for them is service as a religious in His Church. In this case, it matters less if a mother can read and write, but most importantly that she be an upright and genuine Christian. Then, God will surely be abundant in His blessings upon her family.

He holds the Host within the hands
That one-time bore the lights and bell;
Melchisedech, he mounts the throne
Where sounded he the warning knell!..

An Unknown Ingredient

August 27, 1893, fell on a Sunday. In the early morning a pilgrimage made its way to Kevalaer, the famous Marian pilgrimage site on the lower Rhine river in Germany. Among the pilgrims was an older woman who was anxiously anticipating becoming a grandmother sometime over the next few days. She was a good woman. After all—and let's grant the statement the benefit of the doubt—it used to be said that all grandmothers are good. While we can't say there is no such thing as a bad grandmother, there is certainly a lot of good to be found in those mothers who come to love their grandmotherhood. God love and bless our good grandmothers. If goodness alone constituted holiness, may I venture to tease you by wondering if the Holy Father in Rome should, by right, canonize our good grandmothers?! Good grandmothers are a treasure.

So, leave the grandmothers in peace! When the grandchildren, through so much innocent goodness of the grand-

mother, become, perhaps, a little spoiled, so what? The rough
life will make up for it later on. I know a father who once
reproached his mother for "spoiling" his son. She brought
her grandson before him and replied firmly, not without
sharpness: "Do you know that I, with my care, can possibly
bend this boy in eight days, but then you stiffen him again
with your harshness?"

Is the woman not right? One should allow the small ones
the warm autumn sun of grandmotherly love, for quickly
enough the winter of life will break upon them.

Leave the good grandmothers in peace!

Back to our story. There knelt now before the miraculous picture of Kevalaer the woman mentioned before, who
was soon to become a grandmother for the first time. It
weighed heavily on her heart. She herself had given life to
ten children, of whom seven had previously gone to heaven.
Oh, she knew life! But she thought her daughter quite weak.
(Most grandmothers believe that about their daughters, more
or less, while they themselves have perhaps fulfilled their
duty in excess.)

Over and over again on that Sunday morning in Kevelaer,
the woman turned her eyes upon the miraculous picture.
She laid all of her great cares in Mary's motherly heart. Her
rosary was endless that day. She simply wanted to pray without end. She prayed so fervently and well that the dear Mother
of God could not help but let her grace smile upon her, and
under this smile of Mary her first grandchild was born that
Sunday afternoon. But, of course, she didn't know this at the
time and continued to pray fervently.

As the pilgrimage returned that evening, an uncle of the
new grandchild was waiting on the train platform. He went
to the woman, stood before her, laughed, and said, "Hello,
Grandmother!" Startled by his levity, she was dumbstruck

for a moment. In the next moment, the meaning of the greeting came home to her. "Did it all go well? I have prayed so hard...so hard..."

The procession back to the church to end the pilgrimage was beginning to form. The happy new grandmother cried tears of joy which streamed down her face in big drops as she sang out with a joyful heart: "Mary, to love is my wish always..." Scarcely four years later, the good woman died.

It was on that Sunday, August 27, 1893, cherished and cared for by a his holy mother's love, the writer of these lines was born. If on his birthday his grandmother had asked that Mary give him a priestly vocation, it is not known. Is it possible that Grandmother had addressed the matter with her Heavenly Mother? Can we credit her for "secretly negotiating" on behalf of the grandchild? In any case, it is especially worth noting that the grandchild, only three weeks shy to the day of his twenty-seventh year (August 1, 1920), was ordained a priest in the bishop's cathedral church in Luxembourg before the miraculous picture of Our Lady, Comforter of the Afflicted, which is taken from the miraculous picture in Kevelaer.

If a woman wants to have the happiness of seeing her son or grandson as a priest at the altar of God, may she rely on the Mother of the High Priest.

...The white-clad lad whose eyes met mine
As flowered processions proudly passed—
Now, with the Sacred Victim one
Stands on transcendent heights at last!

The Mothers of Priests of Lu

Somewhere in northern Italy is a rural area containing the town of Lu with about four thousand residents. Families with six to ten children are the rule.

In 1881, the mothers of the families of Lu began coming together on the First Sunday of each month to assist at Holy Mass and to receive Holy Communion. What the women brought about by these spiritual exercises is expressed very beautifully in the prayer which they recited together at this Mass. The prayer reads:

> O God, grant that one of my sons becomes a priest! I promise to live as a good Christian woman and will lead my children to all that is good, wherewith I hope to receive the grace to be able to give to You, O God, a holy priest.

So have the women of Lu prayed all these years since 1881. The prayer was short yet so powerful that a flood of priestly vocations were bestowed upon the town. In fifty years, the prayers of these mothers have won at least five hundred priestly and religious vocations from out of the relatively small village. But, remember, it was only in the town of Lu that for those fifty years, the good women were assisting together at the First Sunday Mass specifically for the intention of religious vocations!

Happy, blessed Lu!

The prayers of a mother are indeed powerful when they are intended to beg heaven for priestly vocations. It almost seems that God waits upon mothers for their prayers, and then vocations bloom like flowers in May!

He gives his God unto my heart,
And I who have his life, live mine
In height supreme! He is my gift!
Oh, Mary, what a might was thine!

He passes down the rail from me;
Forever swing our paths apart;
Oh, Mary, what a pang was thine
When God, Thy Son, gave man His Heart!

The Priestly Mother

Today there is a burning question regarding the recruitment of vocations to the priesthood. Much has been said, written, and done in this regard, and with it all there has been too little thinking about the role of mothers with whom, next to God, the almost radical solution lies. If God in His omnipotence can make bread from stones, can call his priests from the most troubled circumstances, though this is at any rate the exception, it proves the rule, that the great majority of all priests owe their vocations not to clever recruitment schemes, but to a good mother or grandmother. The question of priestly recruits is largely a question of the mother, the priestly mother, who transmits the priestly spirit to her sons.

Such a mother places her heartfelt wish before God, praying often and fervently. What the prayer of the mother is capable of doing is demonstrated by the aforementioned mothers of Lu, and even more by the holy Monica, whose eighteen-year prayer for her son—so completely gone to the dogs—won him the priesthood and the episcopacy. Frequently and fervently the priestly mother prays for the great grace of God to call at least one of her sons to the service of the altar. The best opportunities for this mother's prayer are the first seconds after the consecration of Our Divine Lord's Body and Blood at Holy Mass, and after the reception of Holy Communion.

On September 8, 1934, on the Feast of the Nativity of the Blessed Virgin Mary, the parish of St. Hedwig in Berlin, Germany, instituted the first Priest Saturday. This is a parish devotion by which parishioners resolve that on the First Saturday of the month they will receive Holy Communion, sacrifice, and pray the entire day for priests and those who wish to become priests. Since then, the Priest Saturdays have taken on in many places similar status with the Sacred Heart devotion on First Fridays. Mothers praying for the grace of a religious vocation for their sons never miss this devotion so filled with blessings.

It is further advised that mothers, after the example of the Mother of God and such daughters of hers like Alice Rolls and Frau Neuenhofen, consecrate and give their child to God as soon as the child is sleeping in the cradle beneath her heart. Beyond that, the priestly mother must take care there is a genuine Christian family life in her home where aspirations to the religious life are nurtured. Pope Pius XI emphasized the importance of chaste and pious mothers in the nurturing of potential vocations to the priesthood.

Where moral cleanliness rules in a family the love of God and neighbor will be practiced and great joy ensues. Priestly vocations sprout and develop more readily than where the opposite is the case. What a great influence a genuinely

Christian family exercises can be seen from the examples given in this text but also from the results of a poll recently taken of six hundred priests and seminarians in theology. It found that 82% of the fathers and 98% percent of the mothers were "deeply and genuinely pious." And, while 2% of the six hundred fathers were classified "not religious," all six hundred mothers were classed as being at least "religious." Like mother, like son.

Just as the mother provides for a genuinely Christian family, so she must take care that her family is favorably disposed towards priests—let us call this disposition, "priest-friendliness." For a priest to come from a family, a priest-friendly attitude must rule in it. We admit every priest is not a holy Curé of Ars or a St. Vincent de Paul or a Cardinal Mindszenty. We know as well that the priest is human, too, and carries his poor humanity with him always. One should not speak of this before the children. From that family in which the mockery of spiritual things is the order of the day, a priest will almost never come forth. Should a priest stumble, prudent parents will keep watch against all generalization and will pray with heartfelt pity for the poor priest.

From this priest-friendly attitude grows reverence for the priestly dignity. When the parents, and especially the mother, cherish this reverence in their hearts, then it will be easy to plant it in their children. Catholics must look upon the smallest curate and the poorest country pastor with the eyes of faith and recognize they stand higher than all the powers of the earth. "Great is the dignity of the priest," says the *Imitation of Christ*, "that God gave him what He withheld from the angels." The priestly mother takes care that reverence for the priestly dignity has place in her home. Thus may such a happiness bloom in her family and receive a priestly son.

Where a vocation appears to sprout in a family, there a

mother must incubate and nurture it gently with care and attention. It is a completely different thing to coerce or compel a young man into the priesthood. The result would be an immeasurable misfortune. But where, on the other hand, a genuine priestly vocation shows itself, then one must not hinder its development through lazy objections, bantering, or distracting it toward a purely secular life.

Whoever does such things will destroy potential vocations to the priesthood. A mother must have nothing to do with the likes of these.

One may never lay obstacles in the way of a priestly vocation but must further it through a good religious education. When the Church wishes to lead one of her children to Christian perfection, She sends him along the way of the evangelical counsels of poverty, chastity, and obedience. The priestly mother sees in this method of the Church a model for the upbringing of each of her children upon whom God has laid His hand. With solicitude she watches over the associations of the child and holds people, books, and periodicals far from him which could be a danger to the purity of his heart. Furthermore, the education must be carried out in order that the child does not long for extravagance, that he be modestly satisfied with what is necessary, and that through obedience he conquers his own will and follows God without reserve. Thus will a vocation be fostered.

Anytime sacrifice is asked of a family to further a vocation, it is for the most part much more promising.

In order to raise the tuition for his son, the father of St. Vincent de Paul, a small farmer, sold the only work ox he had and pulled the plow across the field himself with his wife and children. The family did this gladly, for as good Christians they knew that the honor of having a priest from amongst them far outweighed the sacrifices. God, however, repaid the high-hearted deed of the family in that the future priest and his brother became great masters of Christian charity, virtually unsurpassed in every land, even to this day.

Powerful as well were the sacrifices of Margherita Bosco and Margherita Sarto for their sons, but they were repaid a thousandfold. Not only was each of them the mother of an outstanding priest, but each was also the mother of a saint. No matter how difficult the sacrifices of a mother of a priest are, the vocation of the son outweighs them all.

There once lived and studied in the seminary of his congregation a young man, Patrick Peyton, who, with the priesthood nearly at hand, suddenly fell sick with galloping consumption. According to the judgment of the doctors, a cure was ruled out. Nevertheless, the student recovered. How was that even possible? Without his knowing it, his mother and sister had offered their own lives in exchange for his. His mother and sister died, and Patrick was ordained a healthy priest. As an extremely holy and precious legacy, Fr. Peyton kept the last letter of his mother in which she had written: "Your mother begged God to be allowed to take on your illness, so that you could get well and become a priest. God has answered your mother's prayer...." Indeed, what noble women are there amongst the priestly-minded mothers of our simple Catholic people!

The priestly mother must take into consideration still one last signpost leading to the great joy of having a son who is a priest. She must be sure the sacrifice she makes be of pure motives. Supposing that he become a secular priest, it is right and by all means in order that one or two daughters run the household for him in order to secure his later life. When, however, a mother sees the priesthood of her son as a way to guarantee a secure life for her girls or to avoid for her girls the anticipated difficulties of possible marriage, it debases the sacrifice to petty dealing so that it is then no longer true, but no more than a cold calculation. The clearest expression of the pure motives of a priestly mother may be found in the mother of Don Bosco, Margherita Ochiena, who said after the First Mass of her son: "You will now pray for me every morning in the Holy Sacrifice. Otherwise, I ask nothing of you. In no way do you need to worry about me. Care first for the souls entrusted to you."

The sincere prayer of a priestly mother, who desires her wish to be that of the good God's, will have the greatest chance of being fulfilled if she fervently and frequently prays for this intention, if she nurtures a Christian family life with constancy and consistency, if she exudes a priest-friendly attitude and a wholesome reverence for the priestly dignity in her home, if she furthers a budding vocation through a good religious training, and when she knows to do all of this with purity of motive and intention.

Afterword

In the year 1950 there was one priest for every 440 Catholics in Switzerland; in Austria, one for every 940; in Germany one for every 1000; in Mexico one for every 5080; in Brazil one for every 6740; and in Guatemala, one for every 18,400. The worldwide average was 1270 Catholics for each priest as well as 5680 non-Catholics and heathens, or about 7000 souls for each priest. (These statistics are worsening.) The crying need for priests in our time cannot be described more clearly or frankly than by these few numbers. How can one priest seriously attempt to direct seven thousand souls? Yes, we have guarantees that the Church, built on the Rock of Peter, cannot be destroyed even though there exists this desperate need of priests everywhere. But the souls are countless who do not find the way to the Catholic Faith because of the lack of priests who should be teaching and baptizing them.

More than ever, the Church needs today the mothers,

those priestly mothers who, priestly-minded themselves, convey their priestly spirit upon one or more sons, just as the noble and great mothers we've spoken about here. The reward of the mother of a priest lies not only in the honor, which, thanks be to God, is still rendered amongst Catholics to the mother of a priest. The mother of a priest also has a share in the priestly efficacy of her son, which he could not practice if she had not mediated, prayed, worked, and sacrificed on his behalf. The mother of a priest receives her full reward above all in eternity.

It will be a great reward.

In the biography of Don Bosco it was related that his mother, Margherita, appeared to him four years after her death. Don Bosco reported the following conversation:

"You, here?! Are you not indeed dead?"

"Nevertheless, I live."

"Are you happy?"

"Indescribably."

"Can you at least give me a small idea of your happiness?"

"Yes," answered the apparition, and in the same instant an indescribable brightness illumined the face of the mother. Her dress began to glow. Incomparable majesty beamed forth from her. A round dance of happy spirits floated around her, a wonderful song rang out, and while Don Bosco took in the blessed picture overpowered and speechless, the mother smiled kindly, and, upon her departure, winking, said: "I wait for you, John; you and I, the two of us, belong inseparably together for eternity."

Prayers

PRAYER FOR VOCATIONS TO THE PRIESTHOOD
(POPE PIUS XII)

Lord Jesus, High Priest and universal Shepherd, Thou
hast taught us to pray, saying: "Pray the Lord of the harvest
to send forth laborers into His harvest" (Matt. 9:38). There-
fore we beseech Thee graciously to hear our supplications
and raise up many generous souls who, inspired by Thy example and supported by Thy grace, may conceive the ardent
desire to enter the ranks of Thy sacred ministers in order to
continue the office of Thy one true priesthood.

Although Thy priests live in the world as dispensers of
the mysteries of God, yet their mission demands that they
be not men of this world. Grant, then, that the insidious lies
and vicious slanders directed against the priesthood by the
malignant enemy and abetted by the world through its spirit
of indifference and materialism may not dim the brilliance
of the light with which they shine before men, nor lessen the

profound and reverent esteem due to them. Grant that the continual promotion of religious instruction, true piety, purity of life and devotion to the highest ideals may prepare the groundwork for good vocations among youth. May the Christian family, as a nursery of pure and pious souls, become the unfailing source of good vocations, ever firmly convinced of the great honor that can redound to our Lord through some of its numerous offspring. Come to the aid of Thy Church, that always and in every place she may have at her disposal the means necessary for the reception, promotion, formation and mature development of all the good vocations that may arise. For the full realization of all these things, O Jesus, Who art most zealous for the welfare and salvation of all, may Thy graces continually descend from heaven to move many hearts by their irresistible force; first, the silent invitation; then generous cooperation; and finally perseverance in Thy holy service.

Art Thou not moved to compassion, O Lord, seeing the crowds like sheep without a shepherd, without anyone to break for them the bread of Thy word, or to lead them to drink at the fountains of Thy grace, so that they are continually in danger of becoming a prey to ravening wolves? Does it not grieve Thee to behold so many unplowed fields where thorns and thistles are allowed to grow in undisputed possession? Art Thou not saddened that many of Thy gardens, once so green and productive, are now on the verge of becoming fallow and barren through neglect?

O Mary, Mother most pure, through whose compassion we have received the holiest of priests; O glorious Patriarch St. Joseph, perfect model of cooperation with the divine call; O holy priests, who in heaven compose a choir about the Lamb of God: obtain for us many good vocations in order that the Lord's flock, through the support and government of vigilant shepherds, may attain to the enjoyment of the most delightful pastures of eternal happiness.

(Partial indulgence.—Sacred Penitentiary Apostolic 11.6.57)

BEFORE THE BLESSED SACRAMENT

O my Jesus, I thank Thee, that Thou art truly, actually, and substantially, human and divine, present here in the mystery of the Sacrament of the Altar.

Thou hast said, "Ask, and you shall receive, seek and you shall find, knock and it shall be opened to you." See, Lord, I come and knock. I ask Thee: Send us holy priests!

O my Jesus, Thou hast said: "Whatever you ask the Father in My Name, it shall be granted you." See, Lord, in Thy Name I ask of Thy Father the grace: Send us holy priests!

O my Jesus, Thou hast said: "Heaven and earth shall pass away, but My Word shall not pass away." See, Lord, in trust of the infallibility of Thy Word, I ask Thee: Send us holy priests!

Most Sacred Heart of Jesus, I trust in Thee! Please, bless Thy priests!

Most Sacred Heart of Jesus, it is not possible for Thee to have no sympathy for us wretches. Have mercy on us sinners, and grant us through the threefold full of grace, beautiful and Immaculate Heart of Mary, Thy Mother and ours, the grace for which we pray to Thee. *Amen.*

PRAYER OF ST. THÉRÈSE OF THE CHILD JESUS

Jesus, Eternal High Priest, preserve Thy priests in the protection of Thy Most Holy Heart, where none can harm them.

Preserve without blemish their consecrated hands, which touch daily Thy Holy Body.

Keep pure their lips, which are reddened from Thy Precious Blood.

Keep pure and holy their heart, which is sealed with the noble sign of Thy Glorious Priesthood. Let them grow in love and fidelity to Thee and protect them from the infection of the world.

Give them with the power of transubstantiation over bread and wine the power of transformation over hearts. Bless their work with bountiful fruit and give them some day the crown of eternal life. *Amen.*

FOR VOCATIONS TO THE PRIESTHOOD

Ant. Why do you stand all the day idle? Go into my vineyard.

V. Ask the Lord of the harvest.

R. That He send laborers into His vineyard.

Let us Pray

O God, who willest not the death of the sinner, but rather that he be converted and live, grant, by the intercession of blessed Mary ever Virgin and of all the saints, laborers for Thy Church, fellow laborers with Christ, to spend and consume themselves for souls. Through the same Jesus Christ Our Lord, Who livest and reignest forever and ever. Amen.

(Partial Indulgence.—Pius X, March 30, 1908)

INVOCATIONS

O Mary, Queen of the clergy, pray for us; obtain for us many holy priests. (Partial Indulgence.—Sacred Penitentiary Apostolic January 16, 1923)

O Lord, grant unto Thy Church saintly priests and fervent religious. (Partial Indulgence.—Sacred Penitentiary Apostolic July 27, 1923)

Send forth, O Lord, laborers into Thy harvest. (*Roman Missal*) (Partial Indulgence.—Sacred Penitentiary Apostolic November 22, 1934)

PRAYER FOR PARENTS WHOSE SON WANTS TO BECOME A PRIEST

Heavenly Father, in childlike faith and trust I come unto Thee, in order to lay before Thee the great desire of my soul. I commend unto Thy Providence my dear son whom Thou hast called, as I dare hope, unto the holy priesthood of Thy Church. What happiness, what a privilege for our family! How can I thank Thee enough for this undeserved favor, for Thy choosing of my child out of thousands to be Thy holy priest! In deepest humility I thank Thee and beg Thee that Thou in Thy great mercy wouldst complete the work Thou hast begun in my son and make him into a priest of Thy Divine Son.

Our Savior and eternal High Priest Jesus Christ, protect my son in all dangers which threaten his vocation during his seminary years. Give him stable health and good progress in his studies. Most particularly I·beg Thee to fill him even now with a truly priestly attitude. Give him a lively and joyful faith, great diligence in prayer, burning love for Thee and Thy holy Church, true eagerness to save souls, deep devotion to the Most Holy Sacrament of the Altar and to the Blessed Virgin Mary.

O good Jesus, make of my son a priest according to Thy Divine Heart!

Holy Ghost, God of Truth and Holiness, pour out over the soul of my son Thy seven gifts. Give him the spirit of wisdom and of understanding, of counsel and of strength, the spirit of knowledge and of piety, and the spirit of the fear of the Lord. Send him Thy divine light in all doubts, courage and confidence in all difficulties, and the power to triumph over all temptations. Holy Spirit, make of my son a worthy and holy priest!

Most blessed Virgin Mary, Mother of the eternal High Priest, be a loving mother and guide for my son on the steep path to the priesthood. Let thy motherly heart always beat for him, thy motherly eyes always watch over him, thy motherly hand guide him everywhere. Stand by him in all the struggles of youth, especially preserve unstained his purity of heart. O good Mother, make my son a priest after the Heart of thy Divine Son!

Saint Joseph, model of priests, take my son into thy special care. Beg for him growth in faith, in hope and in love, in humility, in trust in God and in obedience. Holy Guardian Angel of my son, guard him in all the dangers that threaten body and soul. Lead him safely to the altar of God, "the God Who maketh glad his youth." Saint Aloyisius and all ye glorious patrons of young students, St. Jean Vianney, St. Therese of the Child Jesus, I beg ye all to help my son to preserve his innocence, so that someday he may serve as a chaste and holy priest, in the vineyard of the Lord.

All ye holy Apostles, pray for him! All ye holy Bishops and Confessors, pray for him! All ye holy Priests and Levites, pray for him!

O Divine Savior, bless and sanctify us also, that we may be worthy parents of a future priest. Keep far from our home anything that could damage his priestly vocation. Give our family the spirit of the fear of God, of piety and of Christian morals, so that we be ever more pleasing to Thee and ever more worthy of Thy grace.

Enlighten and bless all those who partake in the education of our son, his teachers and superiors, his confessor and spiritual director, so that they may lead him with wisdom and strength upon the right path to his holy priestly vocation. Bless especially all his benefactors who will help him to attain the priesthood. And finally I pray for all those for whose salvation my son will someday labor. Let him become a sure guide for the souls of many, so that they may attain everlasting life. Amen.

(Taken from *Priestermütter*, the German original of *Mothers of Priests*.)